THE ELEMENTS

Radioactive Elements

Tom Jackson

Marshall Cavendish
Benchmark
New York

Marshall Cavendish Benchmark
99 White Plains Road
Tarrytown, New York 10591

www.marshallcavendish.us

© Marshall Cavendish Corporation, 2006

Library of Congress Cataloging-in-Publication Data

Jackson, Tom, 1972–
Radioactive Elements / by Tom Jackson.
p.   cm. — (The elements)
Includes index

ISBN 0-7614-1923-3
1. Radiochemistry—Juvenile literature. 2. Radioactivity—Juvenile
literature. 3. Radioactive substances—Juvenile literature. 4.
Chemical elements—Juvenile literature. I. Title. II. Elements
(Marshall Cavendish Benchmark)
QD601.3.J33 2005
541'.38—dc21

2005042164

1 6 5 4 3 2

Printed in China

Picture credits
Front Cover: Corbis
Back Cover: Corbis: Walter Hodges

Corbis: 7, Yann Arthus-Bertrand 22, Lester V Bergman 17,
Walter Hodges 5, Roger Ressmeyer 27, Jim Sugar 9
Corbis Royalty Free: 20
Corbis Sygma: Patrick Robert 26
Pacific Northwest National Laboratory: 24
Papilio: Bjorn Backe 13
PhotoDisc: StockTrek 01, 23
Science & Society Picture Library: Science Museum 12, 14
Science Photo Library: US Department of Energy 3, 4, 18
University of Pennsylvania Library: Edgar Fahs Smith Collection 11, 15
US Navy: Photographer's Mate 2nd Class Steven J. Weber 30

Series created by The Brown Reference Group plc.
Designed by Sarah Williams
www.brownreference.com

Contents

What is radioactivity?

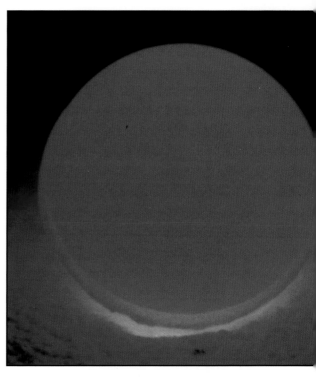

This pellet of plutonium is so radioactive that it is glowing. The glow comes from radiation.

Some elements are radioactive. Radioactivity is a process that occurs when the atoms of an element break apart. As the atoms break apart, they release radiation. The remains of the broken atoms become smaller atoms of a different element.

Atoms

All elements are made up of tiny units called atoms. At the center of an atom is the nucleus. The nucleus contains particles called protons. Protons have a positive charge, which makes the whole nucleus positively charged. Atoms also contain other particles called electrons. These particles move around the nucleus in layers called shells. Electrons are much smaller and lighter than protons, and they have a negative charge. Opposite charges attract each other, so the negative electrons stay close to the positive nucleus.

The nucleus of most types of atoms also contain other particles called neutrons. Neutrons are just slightly larger and heavier than protons. Neutrons do not have a charge—they are neutral.

Although they have charged particles inside them, atoms have an overall neutral charge. This is because they always have an equal number of protons and electrons.

Atomic numbers

There are about ninety elements found on Earth. Each one has a different number of protons, electrons, and neutrons. The number of these particles is what gives an element its unique properties, including making it radioactive.

The number of protons in the nucleus is called the atomic number. The atomic number of each element is unique. The combined number of protons and neutrons in an atom is called the atomic mass number. While the atomic number always stays the same, some elements have atoms with different atomic mass numbers. This is because some elements have a different number of neutrons in the nucleus. Versions of an element with different atomic mass numbers are called isotopes.

Unstable nucleus

Radioactive atoms are unstable because they have lots of protons and neutrons packed into their nuclei. These nuclei are heavy and they break apart easily.

Sometimes only certain isotopes of an element are radioactive. This is because they have too many or too few neutrons in their nuclei. However, the other isotopes of the same element may be stable.

Radiation

When radioactive elements break apart, they release radiation. Radiation is very dangerous because it damages living things. There are three types of radiation. These are called alpha particles, beta particles, and gamma rays. They are named for the first three letters of the Greek alphabet: *alpha* (α), *beta* (β), and *gamma* (γ). Most radioactive elements produce either alpha or beta particles. All radioactive elements also produce gamma rays while they release these other forms of radiation.

Alpha particles are made up of two protons and two neutrons that have broken away from the nucleus. They do not have any electrons, so alpha particles are positively charged.

The radiation produced by radioactive elements is dangerous. This sign is used to warn people where radioactive substances are being used.

ATOMS AT WORK

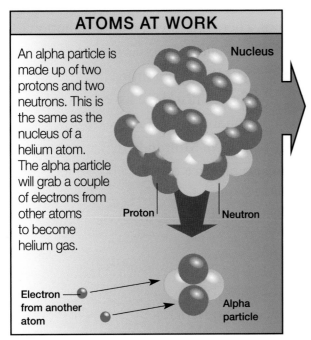

An alpha particle is made up of two protons and two neutrons. This is the same as the nucleus of a helium atom. The alpha particle will grab a couple of electrons from other atoms to become helium gas.

Nucleus

Proton

Neutron

Electron from another atom

Alpha particle

A beta particle is a single electron. The electron is produced when a neutron in the nucleus transforms into a proton.

Nucleus

Neutron

Proton

Beta particle (electron)

If a neutron in a heavy nucleus collapses, it turns into a proton and electron. The electron is released as a beta particle. Most beta particles are single electrons and have a negative charge.

Sometimes a proton turns into a neutron. Instead of releasing a negative electron, the nucleus produces a positively charged beta particle, called a positron. When an electron meets a positron, they are both destroyed.

Gamma rays are a different sort of radiation. They are made of a stream of tiny particles called photons. These are packets of energy and are the same particles that make up rays of light. Gamma rays are a form of invisible light. However, they carry much more energy than the light people can see. Radioactive elements also often release X rays. These are similar to gamma rays but contain less energy.

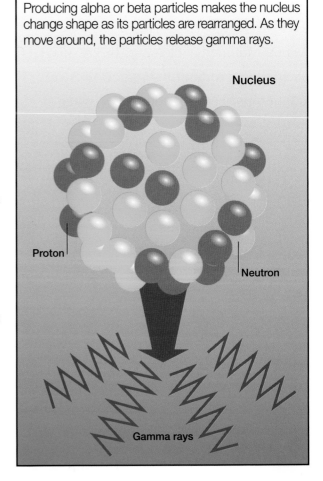

Producing alpha or beta particles makes the nucleus change shape as its particles are rearranged. As they move around, the particles release gamma rays.

Nucleus

Proton

Neutron

Gamma rays

Radioactive elements

There are eleven radioactive elements that are found on Earth. A radioactive element is one that has no stable isotopes. All versions of the element's atoms are unstable and break apart. Many other elements, such as lead

URANIUM FACTS

- Chemical symbol: U
- Atomic number: 92
- Atomic mass number: 238.03 (average)
- Isotopes: U-234, U-235, U-238
- Melting point: 2069 °F (1132 °C)
- Boiling point: 6904 °F (3818 °C)
- Density: 19.05 grams in every cubic cm. (19.05 times denser than water.)

Uranium is radioactive and a very heavy element. This disc weighs nearly 10 pounds (4.5 kg).

and carbon, have a few radioactive isotopes. However, these are very rare compared to their stable versions.

Several artificial radioactive elements have been made in laboratories. These elements are so unstable that many only exist for a few days, or for an even shorter period of time.

Physical properties

Most radioactive elements are metals. These metals are all very dense, and a small sample weighs a lot. The most common radioactive elements on Earth are the metals thorium and uranium. Other radioactive metals, such as radium and actinium, are much rarer.

Three of the radioactive elements found on Earth are not metals. Polonium and astatine are metalloids. (Metalloids share properties with both metals and nonmetals. The most familiar non-radioactive metalloid is probably silicon.) Both polonium and astatine are very rare in nature. For example, scientists think there is just 1 ounce (30 g) of astatine in all of Earth's rocks put together.

Radon is the only radioactive element that is a nonmetal. This element is a gas. It is the only radioactive member of the group of elements called the noble gases. This group also includes helium and neon

URANIUM ATOM

Nucleus

Seventh shell
Sixth shell
Fifth shell
Fourth shell
Third shell
Second shell
First shell

The number of positively charged protons in the nucleus of an atom is balanced by the number of negatively charged particles, called electrons, outside the nucleus. A uranium atom contains 92 electrons. These orbit the nucleus in 7 layers, or shells. There are 2 electrons in the inner shell, 8 in the second, 18 in the third, 32 in the fourth, 21 in the fifth, 9 in the sixth, and 2 in the outer shell.

gas (which are both stable). The noble gases very rarely form compounds. (A compound is formed when atoms of different elements join together.)

Chemical properties

Apart from radon, all the radioactive elements can react with other elements to form compounds. Atoms join together, or bond, by sharing electrons with each other. The way an atom bonds to another depends on the number of electrons it has. When atoms join together in a chemical reaction, they form molecules.

Some radioactive elements, such as francium, are very reactive. As a result they will bond to almost any element. However, when the radioactive atoms break down, the compound also breaks up.

This machine is called a particle accelerator. It is used by physicists to make new types of radioactive elements. So far scientists have made 26 artificial elements that do not exist naturally on Earth.

Decay series

A nucleus breaks apart in a process called radioactive decay. When the atom of one element decays, it turns into an atom of another element. The original atom is called the parent, and the new atom is called the daughter.

Often the parent will decay into a daughter that is also radioactive. As a result, the radioactive decay continues, and the daughter breaks down into yet another type of atom. In this process, the original atom changes from one element to another several times. The long list of these elements is called a decay series.

At each step in the series, the atom loses particles in its nucleus and gradually becomes lighter. The decay series ends

RADON FACTS

● Atomic number:	86
● Atomic mass number:	222
● Isotopes:	222
● Melting point:	−96 °F (−71 °C)
● Boiling point:	−79 °F (−62 °C)
● Density:	0.00973 grams in every cubic cm. (0.00973 times the density of water.)

ATOMS AT WORK

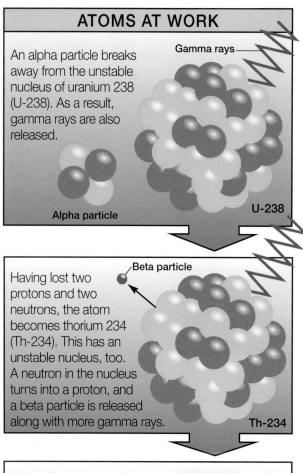

An alpha particle breaks away from the unstable nucleus of uranium 238 (U-238). As a result, gamma rays are also released.

Gamma rays

Alpha particle

U-238

Having lost two protons and two neutrons, the atom becomes thorium 234 (Th-234). This has an unstable nucleus, too. A neutron in the nucleus turns into a proton, and a beta particle is released along with more gamma rays.

Beta particle

Th-234

Now with an extra proton and one less neutron, the atom becomes protactinium 234 (Pa-234). This is a radioactive element, and the decay continues.

Pa-234

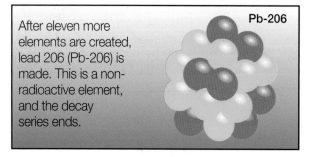

After eleven more elements are created, lead 206 (Pb-206) is made. This is a non-radioactive element, and the decay series ends.

Pb-206

when a daughter element with a stable nucleus is formed. Most decay series eventually produce stable lead atoms.

Half-life

Radioactive elements decay at different speeds. The speed of decay is measured as a half-life. The half-life of an element is the amount of time it takes for one half of the atoms to decay into atoms of another element. For example, imagine 20 ounces of an element with a half-life of one day. After the first day, this element will have decayed into other elements. Half of the original element—10 ounces—remains. After the second day, there will be 5 ounces left, which is half of what was left after the first day.

The most unstable radioactive isotopes have very short half-lives. Some half-lives are less than a second long. The most stable of all the radioactive elements is bismuth. For many years, scientists thought that this heavy metal was not radioactive at all. However, they now know that it has a half-life of 19 billion billion years.

Discovery

Most radioactive elements are so rare that they were only discovered after radioactivity itself was discovered in 1896. However, the two most common radioactive elements, uranium and thorium were identified before radioactivity was discovered.

RADIOACTIVE ELEMENTS

Element	Atomic no.	Isotope	Half-life	Chemical nature
Bismuth	83	Bi-209	19 billion billion years	metal
Polonium	84	Po-209	102 years	metalloid
Astatine	85	At-210	8.1 hours	metalloid
Radon	86	Rn-222	3.8 days	nonmetal (gas)
Francium	87	Fr-223	22 minutes	metal
Radium	88	Ra-226	1,600 years	metal
Actinium	89	Ac-227	21 years	metal
Thorium	90	Th-232	14 billion years	metal
Protactinium	91	Pa-231	32,760 years	metal
Uranium	92	U-234	250,000 years	metal
		U-235	700 million years	
		U-238	4.5 billion years	

Uranium was discovered in 1789 by German chemist Martin Klaproth (1743–1817). He found it in a dark brown mineral called pitchblende. He named the new metal uranium for the planet Uranus, which had been discovered just a few years before. But Klaproth could not figure out how to make pure uranium. Chemists did not make pure uranium until 1841.

Thorium was identified by Swedish chemist Jons Berzelius (1779–1848) in 1828. He named the new element for the Viking god Thor.

Martin Klaproth discovered uranium in 1789. In the same year, Klaproth also discovered zirconium, a non-radioactive metal element. In 1803, he came across another new metal, which he named cerium.

Radioactivity in nature

Invisible radiation is all around us. Most of it is produced by radioactive elements in rocks and the air. Scientists call this background radiation. Usually the amount of background radiation is very low, so it is not dangerous. However, certain rocks contain more radioactive elements, and they produce higher levels of radiation. But only a few rocks produce dangerous amounts of radiation.

Radioactive minerals

By far the most common radioactive elements in nature are uranium and thorium. Nevertheless, these metals are still very rare. Scientists have calculated that there is a third of an ounce of thorium on Earth for every ton of rock (9.6 g per tonne). There is less than one tenth of an ounce of uranium for every ton of rock (2.7 g per tonne).

Uranium, thorium, and most other radioactive elements are found in minerals, such as monazite and pitchblende. Minerals are natural compounds. Earth's rocks are made up of a mixture of minerals.

Pitchblende

The most common uranium-containing mineral is pitchblende. This is a dark brown or black stone. Pitchblende contains uranium oxide (U_3O_8), a compound of uranium and oxygen. The mineral is found in Canada, Australia, the United States, and South Africa. Another uranium mineral is autunite. This forms as large yellow crystals. It is a compound made of calcium, uranium, phosphorus, and oxygen. Autunite is found in Brazil.

Monazite and thorite

Thorium is found in the minerals monazite and thorite. Monazite crystals are yellow brown, and they break up easily. They are made of thorium phosphate ($ThPO_4$), a compound that also includes

Pitchblende is a heavy brown-black rock made up mostly of uranium oxide. The mineral is the main source of uranium and radium.

DID YOU KNOW?

RADIOISOTOPES

Most stable elements have isotopes that are radioactive. These versions of the element are called radioisotopes. Radioisotopes are rare compared to stable isotopes. Most radioisotopes are made by cosmic rays hitting the atmosphere. Cosmic rays are streams of particles, such as neutrons, produced by the Sun and other stars. This radiation bombards stable atoms in the air. Every so often, an atom absorbs some neutrons. This increases its atomic mass number, and it becomes a radioisotope. Some radioisotopes include carbon 14, potassium 40, and tritium (an isotope of hydrogen with two neutrons in its nucleus). Although they are rare, radioisotopes contribute to background radiation.

The aurora, or northern lights, is produced when cosmic radiation hits Earth's atmosphere at the North Pole. (The same thing happens at the South Pole.) This radiation creates radioisotopes.

phosphorus and oxygen atoms. Monazite crystals break into tiny grains and are often mixed up in sand. The mineral is found in India and Brazil.

Thorite is more common than monazite. This dark-colored mineral is made of thorium silicate ($ThSiO_4$), a compound with silicon and oxygen atoms.

Rare elements

Tiny amounts of other radioactive elements are also found in certain minerals. These other elements are made as uranium or thorium atoms in the rock decay. When an element decays into radon, the radon gas is released into the air. Then, as the radon atoms decay, they form radioactive dust.

Discovering radioactivity

Henri Becquerel discovered radioactivity in 1896. He was awarded the Nobel prize for this work.

Radioactivity was discovered a little more than 100 years ago. By studying radioactivity, scientists have been able to figure out how an element's atoms are put together.

In 1896, a French physicist called Henri Becquerel (1852–1908) was doing experiments with photographic plates. These are white plates that darken when light shines on them. Becquerel found that the plates were also darkened by crystals of uranium compounds. He even covered the plates with black paper to stop light from getting to them. The uranium crystals still made the plates dark.

Invisible rays

Becquerel realized that the crystals were releasing rays that made the plates change color. He also discovered that these invisible rays could make gases electrically charged.

Although Becquerel did not understand this, the radiation coming from the uranium was removing electrons from the gas atoms. This is a process called ionization. (An atom that has lost or gained electrons is called an ion. Ions have a different number of electrons than protons. This gives ions an overall positive or negative charge.)

Radiation

In 1898, Polish physicist Marie Curie (1867–1934) began to study how pitchblende was ionizing gases. She and her French husband Pierre Curie (1859–1906) found that pure uranium could ionize gases better than pitchblende. This suggested that the ionizing radiation was coming from just the uranium atoms.

Marie Curie discovered two types of radiation. Although she did not use these names, we now know them as alpha and beta radiation. She showed that a stream of alpha radiation would fly away from a positively charged plate. This suggested that alpha radiation contained positively charged particles that were pushed away

DISCOVERERS

THE CURIES

Marie and Pierre Curie made some of the most important discoveries about radioactivity. They made up the word *radioactivity* to describe what they had discovered. During their research, the Curies discovered two radioactive elements. They noticed that pitchblende was much more radioactive than they expected. They knew that the uranium atoms in the mineral were producing radiation. They realized there must be other radioactive elements in the pitchblende that produced the extra radiation. They began to purify these new elements. Each time they took away one of the elements in the mineral, they found that what was left produced even more radiation. In 1898, they isolated two metals. They named one of them polonium for Marie Curie's home country of Poland. The other metal was was very similar to barium. They named it radium.

by the positively charged plate. (The electrons in beta radiation had been discovered the year before.) A few years later, Pierre Curie discovered a third type of radiation—gamma rays. The Curies suggested that radiation was produced when an atom broke apart.

Atomic research

In 1902, New Zealander Earnest Rutherford (1871–1937) and Briton Frederick Soddy (1877–1965) proved that

Marie Curie (left) and her daughter Irène Joliot-Curie (right). Marie won two Nobel prizes. Irène also won a Nobel prize for her study of radioactivity.

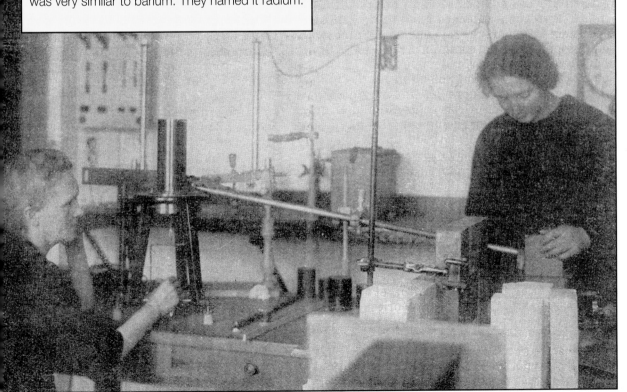

the Curies' idea was true. They showed that a radioactive element changed from a parent atom into a daughter atom of a different element. Rutherford used this research to help figure out the structure of atoms. Soddy went on to discover the element protactinium. He also made up the word *isotope*.

Geiger counter

Radiation is detected by a machine called a Geiger-Müller tube. This is usually shortened to simply Geiger counter. The instrument is named for its inventors. The German physicist Hans Geiger (1882–1945) first made a counter in 1912. In 1928, he and another German, Walther Müller, made a better version.

A Geiger counter can detect alpha and beta particles and gamma radiation. It is made of a metal tube with a thin wire running through the center. The wire is electrified, and the tube is filled with a gas.

Radiation comes into the tube through a plastic window on the end. The radiation knocks electrons off the gas atoms, making positively charged ions. The negatively charged electrons move to the wire and create a pulse of electricity.

A meter counts the pulses, and a loudspeaker turns them into a clicking sound. As more radiation floods into the tube, the number of clicks goes up. An object producing a lot of radiation will make the counter click so much that it produces a steady buzzing noise.

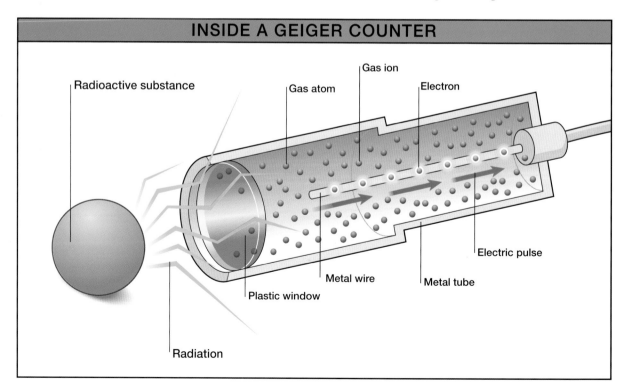

INSIDE A GEIGER COUNTER

Radioactive substance

Gas atom

Gas ion

Electron

Electric pulse

Metal wire

Metal tube

Plastic window

Radiation

Mining and refining

Only the two most common radioactive elements—uranium and thorium—are mined. Most of the other radioactive elements are made from these two metals. Even though thorium is more common, about seven times more uranium is mined each year than thorium. This is because uranium has more uses. It is used mainly as a fuel in nuclear power plants and as an explosive in bombs.

Mining ore

The main uranium ore is pitchblende. (An ore is a rock or mineral that contains a large amount of a useful element.) There are about 3 million tons (2,700,000 tonnes) of uranium ore on Earth. Every year 38,000 tons (35,000 tonnes) of uranium ore is dug up. About a third of all uranium comes from Canada. Other large producers include Australia, Kazakhstan, and Niger. Most U.S. uranium comes from Wyoming.

There are three ways of mining uranium —open-pit mining, underground mining, and solution mining. Open-pit mining involves digging out the ore by producing a huge hole, or pit, in the ground. The ore is carried out of the pit in large trucks. This method is used when the ore is close to the surface.

The sand inside this dish contains monazite, a powdery mineral that is a thorium compound. The sand is producing radiation as the meter shows.

Underground mining is used when the ore is buried much deeper. Miners dig long shafts down to the ore. Then they dig it out producing caverns underground. The mined ore is then hoisted to the surface.

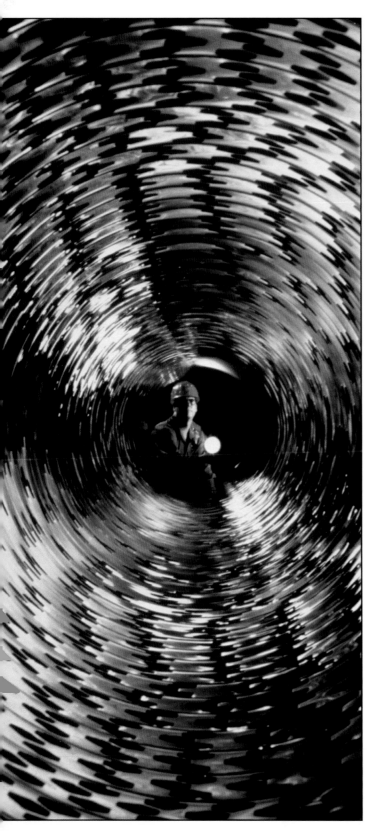

Solution mining does not require any digging. Instead a hot liquid is pumped into the ground. The solid uranium ore dissolves in the liquid to make a solution. (When a solid dissolves, it mixes up with the liquid and disappears.) The uranium solution is then pumped back to the surface.

Refining uranium

The process that makes a pure element from an ore is called refining. The first step in refining uranium is to remove unwanted compounds. This is done using sulfuric acid and hydrogen. A bright yellow powder is left behind called yellowcake. Yellowcake is mainly uranium dioxide. Pure uranium can be made from yellowcake using a chemical reaction. However, few people want pure uranium. Instead uranium is usually sold as yellowcake.

Enriching uranium

Uranium exists in three main isotopes. Nearly of all the uranium atoms in yellowcake are uranium 238 (U-238). However, the most useful isotope is U-235. Less than 1 percent of the refined uranium

An engineer checks the inside of a gas centrifuge used to enrich uranium. This tube is lined with hundreds of holes. It is filled with uranium-containing gas and spun around quickly. The heavier U-238 atoms move out of the tube through the holes, and the lighter U-235 atoms stay inside.

is made up of U-235 atoms. Increasing the amount of U-235 in a sample of uranium is called enrichment.

The first stage in this process is reacting yellowcake with hydrogen fluoride gas (HF) and then pure fluorine (F). This produces uranium hexafluoride (UF_6) gas. The amount of U-235 in this gas is the same as it was in the yellowcake. There are several ways of increasing the amount of U-235 atoms in the gas. One method uses a centrifuge to separates isotopes by spinning the gas. The method used most in the United States is gaseous diffusion.

Diffusion

When a gas is released, it gradually spreads out until it fills the whole space. This is called diffusion. (An example of diffusion is the smells of cooking filling a kitchen.)

Heavy atoms diffuse more slowly than lighter ones. Atoms of U-235 are a little lighter than U-238 atoms.

In gaseous diffusion, uranium hexafluoride gas is made to diffuse. The gas that diffuses farthest and most quickly contains a few more U-235 atoms than the original gas. This process is repeated many times to make a gas that is 4 percent U-235. The uranium hexafluoride is then turned into uranium dioxide (UO_2). Now it is called enriched uranium. The uranium that is left over has less U-235 atoms than normal. It is called depleted uranium.

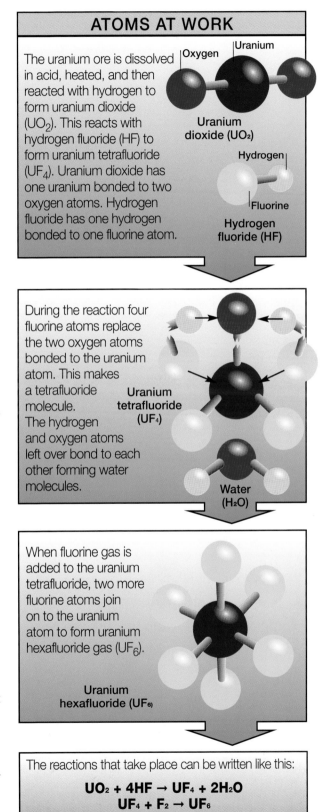

ATOMS AT WORK

The uranium ore is dissolved in acid, heated, and then reacted with hydrogen to form uranium dioxide (UO_2). This reacts with hydrogen fluoride (HF) to form uranium tetrafluoride (UF_4). Uranium dioxide has one uranium bonded to two oxygen atoms. Hydrogen fluoride has one hydrogen bonded to one fluorine atom.

Oxygen | Uranium

Uranium dioxide (UO_2)

Hydrogen |

| Fluorine

Hydrogen fluoride (HF)

During the reaction four fluorine atoms replace the two oxygen atoms bonded to the uranium atom. This makes a tetrafluoride molecule. The hydrogen and oxygen atoms left over bond to each other forming water molecules.

Uranium tetrafluoride (UF_4)

Water (H_2O)

When fluorine gas is added to the uranium tetrafluoride, two more fluorine atoms join on to the uranium atom to form uranium hexafluoride gas (UF_6).

Uranium hexafluoride (UF_6)

The reactions that take place can be written like this:

$$UO_2 + 4HF \rightarrow UF_4 + 2H_2O$$
$$UF_4 + F_2 \rightarrow UF_6$$

Nuclear power

Uranium is the fuel used in this nuclear power plant. The energy the fuel releases is turned into electricity.

Radioactive elements have been used for at least 2,000 years. For example, uranium oxide was used to give glass and pottery a yellow-green color. However, in those days, people did not know that this and other substances produced harmful radiation.

In the nineteenth century, people discovered that uranium compounds glowed in ultraviolet light. (Ultraviolet light is the invisible light that can cause sunburn.) However, after it was discovered that uranium was radioactive and produced harmful radiation, people stopped using it for these purposes. Today the main use of radioactive elements is as fuel in nuclear power plants.

Nuclear fuel

Most nuclear fuel is made from uranium, although a few power plants use thorium. Nuclear power plants make electricity using the heat produced by the radioactive behavior of these elements. Normal radioactive decay makes things heat up. The heat is caused by the radiation smashing into other atoms. However, another type of nuclear reaction produces much more heat. (A nuclear reaction is an event that makes an atom's nucleus change. In a chemical reaction, only the atom's electrons are affected. The nucleus always stays the same.)

Splitting the atom

The heat-producing nuclear reaction is called nuclear fission. The word *fission*, means "to split in two." Nuclear fission is also sometimes described as "splitting the atom." Fission does not happen with all radioactive elements. Only certain isotopes can be used to produce fission. The one used in most nuclear fuels is uranium 235 (U–235).

Nuclear fission is generally caused when an atom is bombarded with particles. Usually neutrons are used to produce fission. If a neutron hits an atom's nucleus, it causes the whole nucleus to split into two or more fission fragments. Each fragment contains roughly equal numbers of protons and neutrons. As the atom splits, it releases a lot of heat and a few single neutrons. Some type of ionizing radiation is also produced, such as alpha or beta particles and gamma rays.

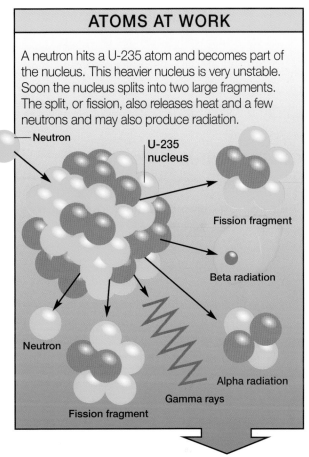

ATOMS AT WORK

A neutron hits a U-235 atom and becomes part of the nucleus. This heavier nucleus is very unstable. Soon the nucleus splits into two large fragments. The split, or fission, also releases heat and a few neutrons and may also produce radiation.

Neutron

U-235 nucleus

Fission fragment

Beta radiation

Neutron

Alpha radiation

Gamma rays

Fission fragment

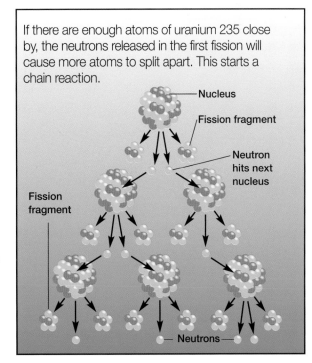

If there are enough atoms of uranium 235 close by, the neutrons released in the first fission will cause more atoms to split apart. This starts a chain reaction.

Nucleus

Fission fragment

Neutron hits next nucleus

Fission fragment

Neutrons

The fission fragments form atoms of new elements, which collect as waste. Radioactive decay always produces atoms of one particular element. However, fission can result in a range of new elements.

Chain reaction

The neutrons released after an atom splits can go on to produce more fission reactions. One split atom can cause

Fission reactions can be controlled inside a reactor. This reactor at a nuclear power plant has been opened to add more nuclear fuel. The reactor core, where fission reactions take place, can be seen under the water.

several more to split. In turn these splitting atoms each result in more fissions of their own. Soon millions of atoms have been split apart. This is called a chain reaction, which produces huge amounts of heat.

If a fission chain reaction is allowed to run at full speed, it produces a devastating explosion. This is what happens inside a nuclear bomb. Nuclear power plants are designed to slow the chain reaction down so the heat is released gradually.

A chain reaction is only possible in samples of uranium that are above a certain size. This size is called the critical mass. The critical mass of a sample depends on how many U-235 atoms are in it.

DID YOU KNOW?

BOMBS

Nuclear bombs produce fission reaction in the same ways as nuclear reactors. The difference is that bombs do not slow the chain reaction, so the atoms all split at once in a huge explosion.

Nuclear bombs use uranium and another radioactive element called plutonium. Plutonium is an artificial element and does not occur in any of Earth's rocks. It is made in nuclear reactors when neutrons are added to uranium 238 atoms in the fuel rods.

The first nuclear bomb ever exploded contained plutonium. This was a test made in New Mexico in July 1945. However, the first nuclear weapon used in war had uranium inside it. This uranium was highly enriched with U-235 atoms. The bomb was dropped on the Japanese city of Hiroshima in August 1945. A plutonium bomb was dropped on Nagasaki, Japan, a few days later. Together, the two bombs killed about 150,000 people and brought World War II (1939–1945) to an end.

A nuclear explosion produces a huge mushroom-shaped cloud.

fuel rod into the rest of the reactor. Some of the neutrons may move into other fuel rods and cause new fission reactions.

Nuclear reactor

Fission reactions are controlled inside a machine called a nuclear reactor. A nuclear reactor is a very large tank of water filled with nuclear fuel.

This fuel is made up of granules of enriched uranium dioxide (UO_2). The granules are packed inside metal tubes, or rods. Each reactor has hundreds of these fuel rods. Fission reactions in the fuel produce neutrons, which travel out of the

In hot water

The heat produced by each fission warms the water surrounding the fuel rods. This water is pumped out and used to turn some more water into steam. This steam spins windmill-like fans called turbines. The turbines are connected to giant magnets inside a generator. When the magnets spin, they make electricity.

There are two parts of the reactor that stop a chain reaction from running too quickly. Between each fuel rod is a substance

Radioactive waste produced by nuclear power plants may one day be stored inside pellets of dark glass. The glass prevents radiation from leaking out.

called a moderator. This slows down the neutrons, so they do not bounce around the reactor too quickly. The moderator in all reactors in the United States is water.

Reactors also have control rods. These are filled with boron. Boron atoms absorb neutrons. The control rods are lowered into the reactor to slow the chain reaction. Raising them lets the reaction run faster.

Waste material

The fuel rods eventually run out of U-235 atoms, and the fission reactions stop. The used fuel is still very radioactive and cannot just be thrown away as garbage. Instead the fuel and other radioactive items from the power plant must be stored for thousands of years to prevent dangerous radiation from escaping.

There have been nuclear power plants for more than fifty years. However, nobody has yet figured out a way of keeping the waste safe for such a long time. Several burial sites are being developed, including one inside Yucca Mountain in Nevada. One likely method will be to bury the waste trapped inside special glass that keeps the radiation in.

Artificial elements

There are ninety naturally occurring elements on Earth. A few other elements, such as plutonium and technetium, were probably present when Earth formed. However, they decayed so quickly that soon none were left.

Physicists have discovered that they can make these elements—and others that have never exisited before—in laboratories. They do this by firing neutrons or positive ions of a certain element at atoms of another natural element. The fired particles smash into one of the natural atoms, and some are absorbed by the nucleus. Because the atom's nucleus has been changed, a new element is formed.

The nuclei of elements made this way are very large and unstable, so they decay easily and have short half-lives. Twenty-six new elements have been made in this way over the last 50 years, but only the first twenty have been given names.

Making elements

Many of the new elements have been named for pioneers in radioactive research. For example, curium was named for Marie Curie and rutherfordium for Earnest Rutherford. Fermium was named for Enrico Fermi (1901–1954). This Italian American built the first nuclear reactor.

Lawrencium is named for American physicist Ernest Lawrence (1901–1958). Lawrence invented the first particle accelerator. These machines can fire particles at huge speeds. Lawrence's accelerator was used to make the first artificial element, technetium, in 1937.

Seaborgium is named for another American, Glenn Seaborg (1912–1999). Seaborg discovered more new elements than anyone else. He helped to make plutonium, americium, curium, berkelium, californium, einsteinium, and mendelevium.

ARTIFICIAL ELEMENTS

Name	Symbol	Half-life
Technetium	Tc	4.2 million years
Promethium	Pm	17.7 years
Neptunium	Np	2.1 million years
Plutonium	Pu	82 million years
Americium	Am	7,370 years
Curium	Cm	15.6 million years
Berkelium	Bk	1,380 years
Californium	Cf	898 years
Einsteinium	Es	472 days
Fermium	Fm	101 days
Mendelevium	Md	51 days
Nobelium	No	58 minutes
Lawrencium	Lr	216 minutes
Rutherfordium	Rf	582 seconds
Dubnium	Db	16 hours
Seaborgium	Sg	21 seconds
Bohrium	Bh	10 seconds
Hassium	Hs	12 minutes
Meitnerium	Mt	0.72 seconds
Darmstadtium	Ds	66 seconds
Roentgenium	Rg	3.6 seconds

Radioactivity and the body

In places filled with radiation, people have to wear protective suits. The thick suit stops any particles touching the skin, and a mask filters out radiation from the air people are breathing.

Radioactive elements are very harmful to the body if they are not handled properly. However, these elements and the radiation they produce are also used by doctors to test for diseases and to cure them.

Health effects

The radiation produced by radioactive elements is dangerous because it ionizes molecules in the body. This can kill body cells and cause cancer. Very large amounts of radiation will burn the skin and cause the body to bleed inside.

Alpha particles are the largest type of radiation, and they cause the most damage to the body. However, because they are so large, it is easier to protect yourself against them. They can be stopped by a piece of paper or clothing. If alpha particles get into the body in food or drink, they can cause a lot of damage.

Beta particles are not as easy to stop because they are much smaller than alpha particles. However, they also cause less damage. Gamma rays will pass through sheets of most metals and cannot really be stopped from entering the body. However, they are less damaging once inside. They often just pass straight through the body.

DID YOU KNOW?

RADIOCARBON DATING

A living body is made of carbon compounds. Living things are always taking in new carbon atoms in food or from the air. A tiny amount of natural carbon is the radioactive isotope carbon 14 (C-14). The proportion of C-14 atoms inside a living thing is the same as the proportion outside.

When a plant or animal dies, it stops taking in carbon, and the amount of C-14 in the body decreases as the atoms decay. Scientists know how quickly C-14 atoms decay. When they compare the amount of C-14 inside a dead body to how much is outside, they can figure out how long it has been since the body died. This is called radiocarbon dating. Things made from wood, wool, and cotton were all once part of a living thing, so they can be dated in this way.

Health benefits

Sometimes doctors put small amounts of radioactive substances into the body. The radiation they produce can be picked up by sensitive scanners outside the body. This lets doctors see structures, such as glands, inside the body that do not show up in X-rays.

The ionizing effect of radiation is also used to kill cancers. Beams of radiation, such as neutrons, positrons (positive beta particles), or gamma rays are aimed inside the body. These beams kill the cancer but do not hurt the rest of the body.

This machine can fire beams of gamma rays inside someone's head. The radiation is used to kill cancers growing deep inside the brain.

Periodic table

Everything in the universe is made from combinations of substances called elements. Elements are made of tiny atoms, which are too small to see.

The character of an atom depends on how many even tinier particles called protons there are in its center, or nucleus. An element's atomic number is the same as the number of protons. Atoms also include particles called electrons and neutrons.

Scientists have found around 116 different elements. About 90 elements occur naturally on Earth. The rest have been made in experiments.

All these elements are set out on a chart called the periodic table. This lists all the elements in order according to their atomic number.

The elements at the left of the table are metals. Those at the right are nonmetals. Between the metals and the nonmetals are the metalloids, which sometimes act like metals and sometimes like nonmetals.

- On the left of the table are the alkali metals. These have just one outer electron.

- Metals get more reactive as you go down a group. The most reactive nonmetals are at the top of the table.

- On the right of the periodic table are the noble gases. These elements have full outer shells.

- The number of electrons orbiting the nucleus increases down each group.

- Elements in the same group have the same number of electrons in their outer shells.

- The transition metals are in the middle of the table, between Groups II and III.

Group I

1
H
Hydrogen
1

Group II

Transition metals

3	4
Li	**Be**
Lithium	Beryllium
7	9

11	12
Na	**Mg**
Sodium	Magnesium
23	24

19	20	21	22	23	24	25	26	27
K	**Ca**	**Sc**	**Ti**	**V**	**Cr**	**Mn**	**Fe**	**Co**
Potassium	Calcium	Scandium	Titanium	Vanadium	Chromium	Manganese	Iron	Cobalt
39	40	45	48	51	52	55	56	59

37	38	39	40	41	42	43	44	45
Rb	**Sr**	**Y**	**Zr**	**Nb**	**Mo**	**Tc**	**Ru**	**Rh**
Rubidium	Strontium	Yttrium	Zirconium	Niobium	Molybdenum	Technetium	Ruthenium	Rhodium
85	88	89	91	93	96	(98)	101	103

55	56	71	72	73	74	75	76	77
Cs	**Ba**	**Lu**	**Hf**	**Ta**	**W**	**Re**	**Os**	**Ir**
Cesium	Barium	Lutetium	Hafnium	Tantalum	Tungsten	Rhenium	Osmium	Iridium
133	137	175	179	181	184	186	190	192

87	88	103	104	105	106	107	108	109
Fr	**Ra**	**Lr**	**Rf**	**Db**	**Sg**	**Bh**	**Hs**	**Mt**
Francium	Radium	Lawrencium	Rutherfordium	Dubnium	Seaborgium	Bohrium	Hassium	Meitnerium
223	226	(260)	(263)	(268)	(266)	(272)	(277)	(276)

Lanthanide elements

57	58	59	60	61
La	**Ce**	**Pr**	**Nd**	**Pm**
Lanthanum	Cerium	Praseodymium	Neodymium	Promethium
39	140	141	144	(145)

Actinide elements

89	90	91	92	93
Ac	**Th**	**Pa**	**U**	**Np**
Actinium	Thorium	Protactinium	Uranium	Neptunium
227	232	231	238	(237)

The horizontal rows are called periods. As you go across a period, the atomic number increases by one from each element to the next. The vertical columns are called groups. Elements get heavier as you go down a group. All the elements in a group have the same number of electrons in their outer shells. This means they react in similar ways.

The transition metals fall between Groups II and III. Their electron shells fill up in an unusual way. The lanthanide elements and the actinide elements are set apart from the main table to make it easier to read. All the lanthanide elements and the actinide elements are quite rare.

Radioactive elements in the table

All elements with atomic numbers higher than 82 are radioactive. There are 11 radioactive elements found in nature, most of which are metals. All of them form compounds, except radon, which is a noble gas. The heaviest natural element is uranium. All elements heavier than uranium have to be made in laboratories or nuclear reactors.

Metals
Metalloids (semimetals)
Nonmetals

								Atomic (proton) number: 92
								Symbol: U
								Name: Uranium
								Atomic mass: 238

			Group III	**Group IV**	**Group V**	**Group VI**	**Group VII**	**Group VIII**
								2 He Helium 4
			5 B Boron 11	6 C Carbon 12	7 N Nitrogen 14	8 O Oxygen 16	9 F Fluorine 19	10 Ne Neon 20
			13 Al Aluminum 27	14 Si Silicon 28	15 P Phosphorus 31	16 S Sulfur 32	17 Cl Chlorine 35	18 Ar Argon 40
28 Ni Nickel 59	29 Cu Copper 64	30 Zn Zinc 65	31 Ga Gallium 70	32 Ge Germanium 73	33 As Arsenic 75	34 Se Selenium 79	35 Br Bromine 80	36 Kr Krypton 84
46 Pd Palladium 106	47 Ag Silver 108	48 Cd Cadmium 112	49 In Indium 115	50 Sn Tin 119	51 Sb Antimony 122	52 Te Tellurium 128	53 I Iodine 127	54 Xe Xenon 131
78 Pt Platinum 195	79 Au Gold 197	80 Hg Mercury 201	81 Tl Thallium 204	82 Pb Lead 207	83 Bi Bismuth 209	84 Po Polonium (209)	85 At Astatine (210)	86 Rn Radon (222)
110 Ds Darmstadtium (281)	111 Rg Roentgenium (280)	112 Uub Ununbium (285)	113 Uut Ununtrium (284)	114 Uuq Ununquadium (289)	115 Uup Ununpentium (288)	116 Uuh Ununhexium (292)		

62 Sm Samarium 150	63 Eu Europium 152	64 Gd Gadolinium 157	65 Tb Terbium 159	66 Dy Dysprosium 163	67 Ho Holmium 165	68 Er Erbium 167	69 Tm Thulium 169	70 Yb Ytterbium 173
94 Pu Plutonium (244)	95 Am Americium (243)	96 Cm Curium (247)	97 Bk Berkelium (247)	98 Cf Californium (251)	99 Es Einsteinium (252)	100 Fm Fermium (257)	101 Md Mendelevium (258)	102 No Nobelium (259)

Reactions

Radioactive elements are involved in two types of reactions: chemical and nuclear. Chemical reactions involve the electrons around the atoms of two or more elements. The reaction rearranges the way these atoms are bonded to each other. At least one new compound is produced by the reaction.

Different changes

Chemical reactions create new compounds, but they do not change the atoms in any way. However, a nuclear reaction does change the atom since it is a change that takes place inside an atom's nucleus. During the reaction, the nucleus gains or loses protons. Therefore, the atom is changed from one element into another.

The nuclear fission reactions of uranium atoms are used to power the engines of large submarines.

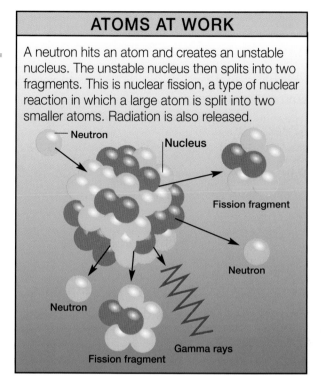

ATOMS AT WORK

A neutron hits an atom and creates an unstable nucleus. The unstable nucleus then splits into two fragments. This is nuclear fission, a type of nuclear reaction in which a large atom is split into two smaller atoms. Radiation is also released.

Neutron

Nucleus

Fission fragment

Neutron

Neutron

Gamma rays

Fission fragment

Writing an equation

Reactions are written down as equations. These show what was there before the reaction and what is there after it.

In a chemical reaction the equation is balanced. The number of atoms before the reaction is always the same as the number after. It is just the order in which the atoms are arranged that changes.

In a nuclear reaction, the equation balances in a different way. The number of particles stays the same, but the atoms change as they lose particles. This equation shows radium (Ra) decaying into radon (Rn) and an alpha particle—made up of two neutrons and two protons:

$$\text{Ra-226} \rightarrow \text{Rn-222} + \text{alpha particle}$$

Glossary

alpha particle: A type of radiation produced when an atom's nucleus decays. An alpha particle is made up of two protons and two neutrons.

atom: The smallest part of an element having all the properties of that element. Each atom is less than a millionth of an inch in diameter.

atomic mass number: The number of protons and neutrons in an atom.

atomic number: The number of protons in an atom.

beta particle: A type of radiation produced when an atom's nucleus decays. Beta particles are generally single electrons. Less often they are positrons.

bond: The attraction between two atoms, or ions, that holds them together.

compound: A new substance made when two or more elements chemically join together.

decay: When a radioactive element breaks down into an atom of another type of element.

decay series: A list of elements that are produced when a radioactive element begins to decay.

electron: A tiny particle with a negative charge. Electrons are found inside atoms, where they move around the nucleus in layers called electron shells.

fission: A type of nuclear reaction that involves an atom's nucleus splitting into two or more large pieces.

gamma rays: A type of radiation produced when an atom's nucleus decays. Gamma rays are a type of invisible light.

ion: An atom or a group of atoms that has lost or gained electrons to become electrically charged.

isotope: A version of an element that has a different atomic mass number than other atoms of that element.

nucleus: The dense structure at the center of an atom.

neutron: A tiny particle with no electrical charge. Neutrons are found in the nucleus of almost every atom.

periodic table: A chart of all the chemical elements laid out in order of their atomic number.

positron: A particle that is the same size as an electron but has a positive charge. Positrons are produced when a proton turns into a neutron.

proton: A tiny particle with a positive charge. Protons are found inside the nucleus of an atom.

radiation: Particles and rays produced when a radioactive element decays.

radioactivity: A property of certain unstable atoms that causes them to release radiation.

solution: When a solid is dissolved in a liquid (the solvent).

Index